The Essential
Book of
CRYSTALS

The Essential Book of
CRYSTALS

PANDORA GEDDES

MOON STONE

First published in Great Britain in 2000 by
Michael O'Mara Books Limited
9 Lion Yard
Tremadoc Road
London SW4 7NQ

ISBN 1-85479-510-4

A CIP catalogue record of this book is available from the British Library

13579108642

Designed and typeset by Design 23

Printed and bound in Great Britain by
Cox and Wyman Limited, Reading, Berks.

CONTENTS

This book is dedicated to the healing and liberation of all beings. May we walk our talk in beauty and love, and step forward together into the New Age?

Thank you Michael, for the blessing of your love and support, and all you continue to teach me.

With special gratitude to Brigitte Ariel, for her amazing inspiration and insight in the crystal realm, and her assistance in the manifestation of this book.

❤

§

A BRIEF
HISTORY OF
CRYSTALS

Everything in the universe, ourselves, plants, the stars above our heads, minerals and crystals, are made of the same basic building blocks. Electrons form into atoms, gather into molecules which build into elements, and everything in life as we know it begins to move from the invisible to the manifest. There is a great similarity in the mineral and chemical elements of all forms of life, whether inorganic or organic, so crystals and humankind have a great deal in common.

Picture the centre of the earth, a huge ball of metallic fire, constantly in motion, constantly pushing gases and liquids upwards towards the surface of the earth. As these liquids solidify in the much cooler temperature of the planet's crust, crystallites appear; pieces of matter with perfect geometric structures, but so small they are invisible to the eye. Under special conditions, where there is room in a vein rich with elements and minerals, these crystallites begin to form into larger crystals and gemstones, varying in colour and shape depending on their composition. Clear quartz crystals have been discovered up to seven feet high.

The mineral kingdom has cast its spell of fascination over mankind since our earliest recorded history. There are references to crystals in the Bible, and crystal structures have been found in the ancient sites of Babylon and Egypt. The great Aztec and Mayan civilisations of Central America are also believed to have attributed special power to crystals, as do the Native North American people. They have been used in the crowns of kings and queens and the priestly classes of many cultures as symbols of their special status and power. Crystals have been worn in armour and breastplates, in the belief that they offered divine protection. Crystals are thought to have been used by our ancestors in magical, ceremonial and healing work and were greatly prized as keys to the mysteries of life. In the last few decades, more and more people have begun to re-connect to these old ways of thinking about and working with crystals.

Quartz crystal (often synthetically grown) is essential in many of our most advanced technologies because of the 'piezo-electrical effect' it exhibits; (the crystalline structures develop positive and negative charges alternately around their edges proportionate in strength to the amount of pressure applied). Quartz is used in computers, ultrasonic sound equipment, radio receivers and transmitters, fibre optics, oscillators (as in our watches), electric guitars (to convert mechanical to electrical signals), amplifiers and more.

The Essential Book of Crystals explores the widely-held belief in the healing potential crystals and minerals offer at this time, and some of the ways they can be used to improve the quality of our lives, and lead us to greater understanding and self-fulfilment. We examine the basic principles of caring for and preparing crystals, and some practical techniques for healing and self-development. These include balancing and clearing the body, mind and emotions, programming crystals for special healing purposes, crystals around the home, meditation, massage, and working with others.

Crystal healing is a subtle and many-layered process and expertise is said to take years of study and dedication. As all journeys begin with a first step, and if one works with clarity, focus and good heart, crystals may provide a unique source of support in our personal evolution.

HEALING
WITH
CRYSTALS

Modern life can be stressful, as we struggle to meet its challenges and develop nurturing and supportive relationships. Sometimes we may feel tired and anxious, or yearn for peace. Perhaps we long to know our true purpose in life or to feel more connected to our spiritual nature. We can find ourselves in a place of dis-ease, and this may lead to unhappiness and possibly ill health. Should we judge ourselves harshly for not being 'perfect', perhaps because of messages we received as a child, this can create disempowering feelings about life and who we are.

In healing, it is important to honour all we may have come through, all we have learnt and experienced, gradually acknowledging that we are beautiful, intelligent and good enough to deserve love and success.

Healing can be seen as bringing the whole person into harmony and out of physical, mental or emotional dis-ease, not just solving an isolated symptom or problem. Crystals are used to enhance this journey by helping clear the 'walls' that may have developed in one's thinking and feeling, so that one can respond creatively and lovingly to life's challenges, rather than reactively and fearfully based on past experience. Healers believe that our minds may be full of mental and emotional conditioning and beliefs about what is 'right' or 'wrong' in others, the world and ourselves. Such conditioning can 'run' our lives and responses, creating conflict within our relationships, and ourselves and blocking us from the heart's true knowing that can guide us to personal and collective fulfilment and evolution.

CONFRONTING CHANGE

Change may bring up fear and cause us to cling to old ways which no longer work for us. It is important to develop trust in one's capacity for healing, and be willing to move on. Crystals are experienced by a growing number of people as powerful tools in the process of change. Strong memories and emotions may be released as healing occurs. Be prepared for this, and know it is part of healing. We may need to re-experience the past to accept it and let go. Such a process needs patience and compassion. But do not expect miracles or instant change, as crystals are believed to work at a subtle level and their effects may take time to show. Ultimately, crystals may help us to transform the way we deal with our spiritual and psychological wounds. Practitioners believe their use can help us to break free from our conditioning and start us on the path to liberation from the prison of our personal history, so that we embrace our truly infinite and eternal spiritual being.

BALANCE AND HARMONY

In crystal healing the stones are used to open channels in our energy that may be closed, blocked, or under or over-energised, helping the body, mind and spirit return itself to balance. The healer merely helps the body heal itself.

Working with crystals is said to enhance one's capacity to channel in the universal life-force, and to ground light into the body, perhaps the most powerful energy in the universe. Remember how light makes nature grow, or picture its strength focused in a laser. Using the beauty of the heart and mind, one can direct this raw potential.

Crystals may help one develop the intuition and knowing within. You can be filled with mystique about crystals, believing all the power is in the stones, but it is believed to be the clarity of purpose and intention the user brings, that is the catalyst for the crystal and the healing.

HOW CRYSTALS WORK AND WHY

At an esoteric level, crystals are believed to influence us through their ability to hold, amplify and send out energy. One theory for how crystals may work is that this vibration sets off a sympathetic resonance within the human energy field, setting it vibrating in harmony with the crystal and its special properties (like the way that plucking one guitar string will set its neighbour vibrating without being touched).

Quartz crystals have been shown to vibrate with incredible precision, and this is believed to raise and 'even out' the human energy field that may be disrupted by thoughts, emotions and life pressures. They are believed to speed up the human vibration, helping us release toxins and ease stress. Crystals also act as de-ionisers, giving off negative ions that can create a feeling of wellbeing in the home.

When the user infuses crystals with his or her clear intentions through the power of will and imagination, it is said this leaves an imprint within the minerals that directs and amplifies their healing potential. This imprint can then be transmitted back to influence our environment and ourselves.

CRYSTAL FORM AND COLOUR
The use of x-rays has shown the inner structure of minerals, and science has found they have perfectly organised geometric forms. These patterns often show in the physical form and number

of 'faces' in a crystal, and are said to bring particular qualities to their energy. In many cultures certain numbers and forms have been thought to carry meaning, and today, the art and science of numerology is growing in popularity. One may sometimes find crystal cut in particular shapes such as circles, pyramids or the six-pointed Star of David to infuse the crystal with more power.

The colour of crystals is thought to be a vital part of their power. Colours are the way our eyes perceive different frequencies of light, and they are believed to have a unique effect. When white light is refracted it splits into the colours of the rainbow, and these colours have been used throughout man's history for their healing potential. Colour therapy is increasingly popular nowadays as we begin to explore more holistic ways of enhancing our lives. Think of the way brightly coloured clothes affect mood, or the colours of a room can soothe or stimulate. What about the way we see 'red' with anger, or feel 'green' with envy? By using crystals of different colours on the body or around the home, one can infuse life with the healing power of colour.

THE POWER OF THE MIND AND IMAGINATION

Crystal healers use the power of their mind and imagination to direct the raw potential of the minerals, and stress the importance of always setting clear and strong intentions.

The power of the mind and imagination is said to be an enormous untapped resource. Yet often the mind may be filled with worries that can work against one.

Crystals may help us to develop more awareness of how our thoughts can shape our experience of ourselves and the world about us, helping us raise the quality of these thoughts to bring the power of the mind to work positively for us.

Everything humanity has created began with an act of imagination. In healing, energy is believed to follow thought, so when clear intentions are set, the healer is trying to empower, focus and direct the crystals towards a particular purpose. Healers may set the intention for the crystals to work at a physical, emotional, mental or spiritual level of a particular issue or a person's energy.

It is vital to have a clear aim in crystal healing. Setting an intention doesn't need to be complicated. Once you have decided how you wish the crystal to assist you, sit quietly and take a few deep breaths. Put the troubles of the day away and relax, bringing yourself into the present moment. Just be aware of your breath entering and leaving your body, don't do anything. With each out-breath, let go a little more. Many people like to say a small prayer and ask for a blessing at this point, according to their beliefs. Now, state your intention, visualising it manifesting in your life. Try to keep the focus strong and clear. This should get easier with a little practice.

It is a principle in all forms of healing never to set intentions that interfere with the freewill of somebody else, and that the work be for the good of all beings.

Let love empower all your work.

CRYSTAL HEALING AND THE HUMAN BODY: THE CHAKRA SYSTEM

One of the principle ways crystals are used in healing is the 'laying on' of stones over the *chakras* or energy centres of the body. These centres are associated with different colours, qualities and attributes. Many healers claim to see these centres as spinning discs of light, each a different colour of the rainbow. *Chakras* are said to co-ordinate our physical, emotional, mental and spiritual natures, affecting all levels of our being and connecting us to universal energy. They may react strongly if we experience upset or trauma, becoming closed, congested or out of balance. Crystals are used to clear these centres and harmonise their interaction. One of the main reasons that the colour of a stone is considered important is because of its resonance with the same coloured *chakra*. Here is a brief description of the location and qualities of these centres:

৯ৎ

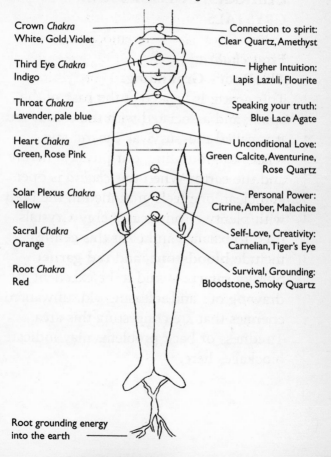

Connection to Spirit and Higher self

Crown *Chakra*
White, Gold, Violet

Third Eye *Chakra*
Indigo

Throat *Chakra*
Lavender, pale blue

Heart *Chakra*
Green, Rose Pink

Solar Plexus *Chakra*
Yellow

Sacral *Chakra*
Orange

Root *Chakra*
Red

Connection to spirit:
Clear Quartz, Amethyst

Higher Intuition:
Lapis Lazuli, Flourite

Speaking your truth:
Blue Lace Agate

Unconditional Love:
Green Calcite, Aventurine,
Rose Quartz

Personal Power:
Citrine, Amber, Malachite

Self-Love, Creativity:
Carnelian, Tiger's Eye

Survival, Grounding:
Bloodstone, Smoky Quartz

Root grounding energy
into the earth

CHAKRAS, COLOURS AND CRYSTALS

First *chakra*:
The Root - Grounding:
This centre is located at the base of the spine, and associated with the colour red. It is called the 'survival' *chakra*, and relates to grounding, our physical nature and the earth. When this *chakra* is open and clear, one feels grounded in the body with plenty of physical energy. Crystals used to balance and clear this centre include **bloodstone**, and **red garnet**. **Smoky quartz** is said to be excellent at drawing out and releasing old, unwanted energies that are congesting this area. Tiredness or back problems may indicate blockages here.

§

Second *chakra*:
Sacral Centre - Self-love:
This centre sits a couple of inches below
the navel, and is associated with orange.
It relates to our sense of self-worth, how
we express ourselves creatively and
sexually, and the capacity for pleasure
and sensuality in our relationships to
each other and the world. This side of
one's nature may have been shamed or
repressed in childhood, causing one to
lose touch with the fire of creativity and
sexuality. **Tiger's eye** is used to help
open this centre and give the courage to
be oneself. This stone is believed to
show us the earthy beauty of the
sensual self, helping relaxation and
acceptance of our physical nature.
Carnelian is a red-orange stone that
healers use to fire up this centre,

helping dissolve old hurts to the sense of self. Difficulty expressing creativity, or a feeling that you don't have the right to let go and enjoy life, may indicate blockages or imbalance here.

∾

Third *chakra*:
The Solar Plexus - Personal Power:
This *chakra* is located just above the navel and its colour is yellow. It is said to be the sun in our body, the place of our sense of individuality and power and its expression in the world. Since childhood, we may have learnt to give away our power to avoid disapproval, eventually finding it difficult to know what we want and how to assert ourselves appropriately. Lack of

confidence and motivation, or finding it hard to believe in yourself, may indicate difficulty with this centre. Crystals used here include **citrine**, **amber** and **malachite**. Work very gently with **malachite**, as it is considered very powerful in bringing up suppressed emotion, and it is wisest to release such energies gently over time.

~

Fourth *chakra*:
The Heart - Unconditional Love:
This centre is in the middle of the breastbone in line with the heart, and is associated with the colours green and rose pink. It is said to connect us to the oneness of life, and to open us to unconditional love, for ourselves and all

of life. This *chakra* is easily affected by any hurts we may have received in life, and can react by closing down to protect itself. Working here one may experience old sadness and anger, so again it is recommended one works gently, staying aware and integrating changes slowly. Crystals used at the heart include **green calcite**, **green aventurine** and **rose quartz**.

∽

Fifth *chakra*:
The Throat - Speaking Your Truth:
This centre is at the throat just above the collarbone. It is associated with lavender or pale blue. It is known as the centre of communication and speaking one's truth and essence.

Difficulty verbalising or even being aware of your individual truth, or frequent coughs and sore throats, may be due to suppressing emotions and containing them here for fear of not 'fitting in'. All the pale blue stones are used here to help move through these fears, to openly communicate your truth. Many healers especially favour soothing **blue lace agate** for its gentle and loving action.

Sixth *chakra*:
The Third-eye - Seeing Clearly:
This *chakra* lies between the eyebrows, and its colour is indigo. It is thought to be the centre that determines how we perceive reality, the home of our higher

intuition and psychic senses. Experiencing a lot of fear in life, without a specific cause, has been said to indicate a blockage or overactivity. Sometimes relief of headaches or migraines, if they are due to excess energy, can be found by working on this centre. Stones that are used here include **lapis lazuli**, **amethyst** and **purple fluorite**.

Seventh *chakra*:
The Crown - Connection to Spirit:
This centre is at the top of the head, associated by some with violet and others with white or gold. It is said to relate to our spiritual nature, and our connection to cosmic energy. It is

through this centre that we draw spiritual force and light into our beings, and connect with our higher selves in meditation. Crystals used here include **amethyst** and **clear quartz**.

THE HUMAN AURA

Healers believe the human energy field or 'aura' also contains different layers of energy from the gross physical to the very fine. The 'aura' is said to be made up of physical, mental, emotional and spiritual bodies, sometimes seen by healers as egg-shaped sheaths around the physical body. It is believed that a problem that is finally manifest physically will often have begun at another level of the aura. Crystal healing will often work on a particular 'body' of the aura, depending on a client's needs. This is an aspect that is considered when programming and laying on stones, and as more experience is gained, intuition is often the best indication as to which level to address.

SOME ESSENTIAL HEALING CRYSTALS

There are many different crystals from which to choose when you begin a collection. Some people prefer to buy one or two at a time, adding more as they become familiar with them. How about buying one stone for each of the energy centres or '*chakras*'? This will form a useful basic set of crystals with which to explore some of the healing suggestions in later chapters. Crystal healers tend to have their personal favourites; those that they feel work best for them. Everybody will discover those that appeal most to them through handling and working with the different stones. The following are a selection of crystals commonly used in healing, some working particularly well with certain centres. These crystals should be readily available and

inexpensive to buy. You may come across
them in their raw state, or polished and
faceted; choose those that appeal to you.

∾

Amethyst
(Crown and Third Eye *chakras*):
Amethyst is a form of quartz. As it
contains manganese and iron, it ranges
in colour from purple to pale violet. It is
said to encourage peace, harmony and
spiritual expansion. Many healers believe
it is capable of gently purifying,
balancing and stabilising the body,
emotions and mind, helping one to 'let
go' and trust in times of change or
transition.

It is often worn for its protective

qualities, and is said to deflect negativity, helping the user to stay calm and relaxed when stressed or overworked. It is popular worn as jewellery because of this. It is said to bring wisdom and awareness from the higher self into our lives, and is often used in meditation, to access higher truth. It has been used to strengthen the skeletal system, and to relieve insomnia, headaches and mild depression. It is recommended as a comforter in times of change or loss. It is one of the principal stones used to clear and activate the crown and third eye *chakras*.

Blue lace agate (Throat *chakra*):
This beautiful crystal is pale, lavender blue with soft white banding. It is most often used at the throat *chakra*, encouraging the release of old patterns of learned inhibition and constriction, and helping to activate this centre so you can rediscover and express your truth. It is used in working on problems associated with blockages in this area, such as neck and shoulder aches, headaches and sore throats. It has also been used in the treatment of arthritic problems.

It is recommended as a wonderful stone to wear or keep in a pocket to assist in peaceful expression of your truth as you go about your day. It is said to help to access higher states of awareness and to express these clearly. It might be called 'the stone of truth'. It is prized for its gentle, peaceful, cooling energy, and some healers recommend it as a powerful antidote at times of heated anger or upset.

Carnelian (Sacral *chakra*):
Carnelian is an agate, and comes in a variety of hues between red and light orange. Its warm colour may be naturally soothing for stressed or confused minds and emotions. It is thought to activate natural talents and mental abilities, and to be excellent for improving concentration. It has been used to counteract passivity, and to

help to manifest effectively in the physical world. It is often made into exquisite carved jewellery that can be worn to keep focused and grounded. It is said that it can build a bridge between the physical and spiritual and increase energy and creativity. Because **carnelian** is believed to help purify the blood and reproductive organs, it is often used at the Sacral *chakra* to clear and activate it, helping release fears that may be stopping the expression of natural creativity and sensuality.

~

Citrine (Solar Plexus *chakra*):
Citrine is a form of **quartz** that ranges in colour from light yellow or gold to burnt orange. Some healers say it is a

stone that does not hold negative energy. It is traditionally thought to be effective in attracting and maintaining wealth, encouraging the release of the fear of lack. Some sources warn that if this stone is used for selfish ends, it will lead to unhappiness. It is said to develop the capacity for mental clarity. Its colour is reminiscent of the heat and rejuvenating power of sunlight, and it is often used to 'lift the spirits' and increase optimism. It is favoured to clear, activate and energise the solar plexus. Blockages in this area may manifest in digestive, kidney, or bladder problems, and this crystal is used to relieve congestion and emotional disturbances, leading to increased self-belief, confidence and esteem. It is used to channel the revitalising golden ray associated with the crown *chakra* into the body, helping those who work with it to express their personal power with integrity. Recommended for its protective influence, it is often worn by those who are very sensitive and easily buffeted by the outside world.

❧

Clear quartz:
Quartz is used in many ways in healing, meditation and spiritual development. It is known as a purifier of energy at all levels. It is said to be able to bring stagnant energy to the surface, which it is then able to release. It is used to clear and re-charge the *chakras*. It is prized as a crystal for dispelling darkness and negativity.

Quartz is believed to hold, amplify and emit energy, often being 'programmed' with the user's healing intentions, which it then reflects back to them and out into the world. It is thought to strengthen the immune system, and to encourage self-healing. It has a very precise vibration, and for this reason it is thought to bring whatever is around it into greater harmony, whether in a room or a person.

QUARTZ
Clear quartz carries all the colours and may bring the purest form of these colours and their healing potential into your energy field. Meditators prize it to help connect to their higher selves, and encourage the growth of awareness. It may be used at the crown *chakra* to

open and activate it, and to usher healing white light into the body.

Clear quartz comes in many varieties from single points with different configurations or 'faces' at their termination, to large clusters. All are said to carry special qualities that can be made use of in healing and self-development. The following are a few of the most commonly used in healing:

Single terminated quartz is the most commonly found, with six sides and one end that comes to a point, made of 'faces' of different shapes. It is often used in crystal healing to charge and discharge energy from the body. Single **quartz** is often used at the crown *chakra*, with the point resting against the top of the head, to help bring in the pure light of spirit.

❧

Double-terminated quartz have points at both ends. It is best that they are naturally formed, rather than cut to this shape. These **quartz** are said to open the energy flow between two points, and can be used to draw in and put out energy from both ends. They are often used in *chakra* layouts to help the energy flow between the centres, so that too much in one and too little in another can balance out, and harmony between them be achieved. Double-terminated **quartz** is said to help in dream recall and meditation.

Generator quartz has a single termination where all six faces are of a similar shape and meet in a sharp point. These may be more difficult to find, and are believed to be the most powerful **quartz** for generating and directing energy, and for charging other crystals.

❧

Quartz clusters consist of many small single terminators pointing out in different directions. These clusters can be used for cleansing and energising a space, other crystals and jewellery. Place them gently on for as long as necessary. They are thought to carry a strong healing vibration, and can be used in a space that may feel disturbed after an argument or upset. These clusters are said to be self-cleansing, but it is probably best to clean them if they appear to need it.

❧

Rainbow quartz Some **quartz** will contain beautiful patterns of rainbow colour when held to the light. These are said to be 'happiness' crystals and can be used at times of sadness or loss. They are wonderful to meditate with, when you can breathe their colour into your heart and mind.

❧

Channelling quartz has one seven-sided face at the front, with a triangular face at the opposite side. These crystals are supposed to help channel information from the highest sources during meditation and healing. They are also thought to develop clarity and wisdom through accessing the higher self within. Many healers suggest one should call for protection and guidance in using these powerful crystals, setting a clear intention that the work be for the good of all.

❧

Rutilated quartz contains rutile needles of different colours. **Rutile** is believed to repel negativity and assist in getting to the root of a problem. It is known as a stabiliser of imbalances. When **rutile** and **quartz** combine, they are believed to intensify the power of each other. This produces a crystal that is able to access and clear strictures and difficulties at the deepest level.

❧

Rose quartz (Heart *chakra*)
Known as the stone of love, **rose quartz** is prized for its calming, nurturing energy, and frequently for healing the wounds of the heart. It is said to help forgiveness and letting go of the past. It releases sadness and loneliness so that you rediscover self-love and honour the lessons that have been learnt. At the Heart *chakra* it is used to penetrate suppressed pain, allowing re-connection with the capacity for unconditional love, infusing the centre with soft and gentle comfort and a sense of security.

It is recommended as an excellent crystal to simply sit and hold at times when we feel unloved or unable to give love. It has been used in the treatment of high blood pressure, vertigo and headaches, as its calming energy appears to reduce anxiety. It is a popular stone for meditators, centring the mind and emotions prior to entering higher states of awareness. It is loved in jewellery as soothing to wear in stressful situations.

❧

Smoky quartz (Root *chakra*)
Smoky quartz ranges in colour from black to the palest grey. Its colour is due to natural radiation during its growth. Even the darkest **smoky quartz**

will appear transparent when held to the light. It is used for drawing out and dissolving blockages and negative energy, allowing more positive influences into the body, emotions and mind. It is said to be a wonderful stone for 'keeping your feet on the ground', helping to stay alert and focused.

Smoky quartz is used to help in 'manifesting' dreams. It works slowly and gently to release what we no longer need, while keeping us balanced and protected. It may be helpful for those who are trying to let go of old hurts. It is associated with the Root *chakra*, and believed to be effective at clearing and activating this centre, but is also used on any part of the body to dissolve impurities.

These crystals will provide a good set to gently begin healing work. However, you may also like to consider some of the following stones much valued by crystal healers.

❧

Amber

Amber is actually fossilised tree resin. It may be gold to deep reddish-brown. It is said to have the power to draw out disease and imbalance from the body, absorbing negativity and stabilising energy. It is grounding and soothing to wear. It can be used over any part of the body, but is particularly used around the sacral and solar plexus areas to energise the digestive and reproductive organs.

Azurite

This is a very powerful stone, its colour ranging from light to deep indigo blue. Known as a very strong mover of energy, it can be used anywhere on the body to bring up unresolved and unconscious patterns, physical, emotional or mental. It may lead to powerful emotional releases. It is often used at the throat and third eye to help clear these areas, helping access to and the expression of your highest spiritual truth.

☾

Bloodstone

Bloodstone is an earthy crystal of deep red and green. It is said to powerfully cleanse the physical organs and body, detoxifying the blood and organs, and helping with circulation. It is usually used at the root and sacral *chakras*.

§

Calcite
Calcite comes in many colours and forms. It is known as a healer and balance on the mental level, helping us to let go of old ideas and accept new ones. It has been used with those feeling stressed or anxious, especially in times of change. **Calcite** of the appropriate colours can be used at different *chakras* to clear and activate them. **Green calcite** has been used to treat arthritis and rheumatism, and is said to help in the release of fear. It is often chosen as a meditation stone.

ॐ

Fluorite
Fluorite can be found in blue, purple, white, gold, pink and green, and can manifest in clusters, pyramids and octahedrons. It is said to have a peaceful, calming effect, assisting an experience of oneness with the universe. It is used to stabilise and regenerate energy, bringing order out of disorder to achieve a state of equilibrium. Depending on its colour it can be used at different *chakras* for purification and balancing. It is often used at the third eye. The pyramid form is particularly prized as a meditation aid.

❧

Green Aventurine

This is a beautiful pale green stone that may sparkle with the small inclusion of mica. Its healing green ray is said to soothe and balance. It is particularly prized for working on the heart area to help melt any hurts that may be constricting this *chakra*. It is gentle, but penetrating in its effect. It is said to work wonderfully with **rose quartz**.

Malachite

Malachite is a powerful green stone, and may be marked with rings and lines. It is known as an emotional purger, bringing to awareness suppressed energy, and mirroring this back to the user. It can be placed over any part of the body, but is often favoured at the solar plexus. Its use can lead to powerful emotional releases and physical detoxification. **Malachite** is often used in conjunction with a crystal, such as **clear quartz**, that can disperse the energy it raises.

❧

Tiger's eye
Tiger's eye is a form of **quartz**, with bands of gold and brown. It carries both the energy of the golden ray of the crown and the earthiness of brown. It has been called 'the stone of courage', and is often used at the first, second and third *chakras* to usher in and ground higher awareness into the body. It is thought to be very grounding,

giving strength of purpose and helping to move forward, even in difficult times. It is used to encourage a feeling of wellbeing, relieving nervousness or lack of confidence. It is said to help the enjoyment of sensual and physical being as a part of one's divinity.

Tourmaline
Tourmaline comes in many colours, each with a special affinity for particular *chakras* because of its colour. It is said to be purifying and protective, repelling negative energy and acting to clear and stimulate the body, emotions and mind. **Green tourmaline** is said to counteract fatigue and inspire creativity; **black tourmaline** to deflect unwanted

energies. **Pink tourmaline** is often used at the heart *chakra* to inspire one to release the past and joyfully embrace the present.

Remember, trust your own feelings and select those stones that you are drawn to even if they are not mentioned here. It is a good idea to check on their properties before using them, as some stones are thought to be very powerful and it is best to begin gently. Crystal sellers often have their favourite sourcebook on or behind the counter, and they will be happy to let you use it, or offer help and advice.

৭৯

GATHERING
AND
PREPARING
CRYSTALS

CHOOSING CRYSTALS

Crystals may be given as a special gift, or beautiful stones and colourful pebbles can be discovered as you wander through the countryside or along the coastline. Many shops specialise in selling crystals, and this is a wonderful way to start collecting. It is best to choose in person, as the relationship between the crystal and its user is very individual, and it gives one the opportunity to spend time with different stones, tuning in and exploring their colours and shapes.

Before going into a crystal shop it is a good idea to ground oneself. Crystals are bounding with energy, and some people may find it a bit overwhelming, like going into a room full of people all wanting one's attention! A good way to prepare is to close your eyes, take a few deep breaths, and imagine roots growing out through your feet into the centre of the earth. Feel the strength of the root, the way it anchors and supports you. This exercise need only take a moment before entering the shop.

Don't feel rushed or intimidated into buying something. Crystal sellers are often experts, and love to help and answer questions, and they will expect people to take their time. You may like to acquire a few stones at first, working with these for a while and building your collection slowly. It is important to feel a connection with the crystals you buy. This may be experienced in different ways when holding a stone: a buzzing or tingling in the hands, energy moving in different parts of the body, a sense of joy or bubbling happiness, sensations of heat or cold, images or colours in the mind's eye. Some people simply feel the stone is 'right' for them, or find themselves strongly attracted to the colour, texture or shape. It is said that the stone you choose is always the right one, so trust your intuition.

Some people are strongly drawn to a crystal without knowing why, and such a stone is said to have 'found' them. Its purpose becomes clear as it is worked, or perhaps when it is used in meditation. If you are looking for a crystal for a particular purpose, which may often be the case, it is important to set a clear intention to guide your choice.

After grounding yourself, simply close your eyes, and focus on your intention, imagining the crystal working in this way. There is tremendous power in the mind and imagination, so trust this. This power is fundamental in crystal healing work.

An intention may be simply that the crystals you are meant to work with at this time make themselves known, or it may be more specific, such as finding a stone to help you meditate, relax, or work on a certain project or type of healing. Some people like to request that any other crystals remain quiet while they choose.

It is important to let yourself 'feel' the way, and not to try and work it out with the head. You can ask for guidance or a blessing according to your beliefs. Open your heart, relax and play. Have a look around and pick up any crystal that attracts you. Hold it in both hands (some people feel more through the left hand, which is said to be more receptive to subtle impressions). Do you like the colour, the shape, and the feel of it? Examine it closely, looking for any marks or inclusions. Some people experience crystals as literally coming to life in their hands, getting more bright or colourful, or showing rainbows as they become activated. Many people feel very little if anything when they begin working with crystals. This is quite normal. The crystals are said to work and respond to our intentions whether we feel it or not. Some people like to ask the crystal if it is the right one for them, for a particular purpose, or for a certain friend. Listen with the heart, and trust any answer you receive. If you feel unsure, leave the shop for a while and come back later. Some people find a crystal will 'call' to them while they are away, and prize these as having 'found' them.

It is a good idea to decide how much you can afford to spend before buying crystals, as it can be easy to get carried away with enthusiasm. Bear in mind that crystals do not need to be big or expensive to work well, especially when you first begin to work with them.

↩

CLEANSING AND CLEARING CRYSTALS

From being mined, through wholesalers, shops and others users, a crystal will have taken a long journey on its way to you, and is likely to have absorbed all kinds of energies, influences and imprints. Remember, crystals are believed to attract, store and release energy. It is considered important to remove any unwanted influences from minerals when they are first acquired and to continue to cleanse them regularly. Once a week is recommended for general maintenance. Crystals will also need cleansing if they have been put away for a while, after they have been in a highly charged environment (for example a room where a row has occurred), and before and after using them for healing. When it looks dull or feels sticky your crystal needs cleaning. Some people may experience a shooting pain in the hand or a slight headache when picking it up.

There are many ways to cleanse crystal, and everyone develops their favourites. Whichever method you choose, it is considered vital to set a clear intention first. For example, you could say, "May all unwanted energies be released through Divine Will and for the good of all beings". Focus on cleansing the stone, imagine the unwanted energies being released to the core of the earth or sun (it is important to direct the energies somewhere) in the form of cloudy smoke or water, and the crystal filling with radiant light.

Many crystal healers use the power of nature and the four elements for cleansing. Some crystals have a natural affinity with water, while others like **azurite, malachite** and **calcite** are hydrophobic. Ordinary tap water is fine for everyday use. As you say your intention, hold the crystal under the tap with its termination facing down (if it has one), and visualise any unwanted energy draining away. Wash the crystal until it feels cleansed (a couple of minutes should be enough). When by a stream or the sea, place small crystals in an old knotted sock that can be weighed down and let them soak. A basin of water, with some natural salt or a few drops of Bach Remedy Crab apple is meant to work well.

Passing a crystal quickly across a candle flame while imagining unwanted energy leaving it is said to be effective. Don't hold the crystal in the flame, as strong heat may damage it. A popular way of using the element of fire is to use 'smudge'. This is a mixture of herbs used by Native North Americans and those who follow their shamanic teachings, who have a long tradition of using crystals for healing and self-development. The herbs may include sage, cedar or sweetgrass. You can often find 'smudge' where you buy crystals. Place some herbs in a safe container, a small shell makes a beautiful one, and light them. Hold the crystal over the smoke while saying your intention. You can use incense in a similar way.

Some people like to bury crystals in the earth to cleanse them. Darker crystals, such as **smoky quartz** or **obsidian** may prefer this, or any stones that have worked very hard or been exposed to extreme stress. A corner of the garden, or a window box is fine. Take care to bury them gently, protecting any terminations. It is best to bury them for a minimum of two days, and a maximum of a week if they are really in need of rest.

You can also use the power of the breath. Inwardly saying the cleansing intention, simply breathe love and light into the crystal, imagining as you do the breath pushing out unwanted energy to the core of the sun or earth, and replacing it with pure light.

CHARGING AND ENERGISING CRYSTALS

Crystals may become tired and burnt out through working hard. Like a battery or car engine, they are believed to need recharging and 'fuel' to continue working effectively, and it is important to provide them with energy after cleansing them.

Smudge, incense, sound, thoughts of love and light, and spending time in nature are some of the ways people re-energise their crystals. Giving them plenty of sunlight and moonlight is recommended, as it is believed they will draw the regenerating power and life force of nature into themselves. Certain coloured stones, however, do not like long exposure to sunlight, as it is known to affect their colour. These include **amethyst, rose quartz** and **citrine**. A few hours sunlight is fine. Never keep any crystal in darkness for long periods.

If they appear dull, or their colour is fading, or you feel intuitively that they need a boost, why not ask them what they would like and trust the answer received? Smaller crystals can be placed on a **quartz** or **amethyst** cluster to cleanse and energise them. Why not try playing them some inspiring and beautiful music?

Healers believe crystals to be sacred, conscious and living beings, and treat them as such. A simple square of silk or soft cloth can be placed in a quiet corner of the home to make a sanctuary for them. Take great care of crystals when they are being moved, as they can be very easily damaged, and wrap them carefully when travelling.

ATTUNING TO CRYSTALS

Tuning in to crystals is done to establish a personal bond, as with a new and valued friend, so energy can move easily between the user and the crystal, and communication at a subtle level can be opened. It is said to allow the user and the crystal to 'key' into one another's energy.

One way to do this is to close your eyes, open your heart and go within. Introduce yourself to the crystal, and let it talk to you. Listen without straining,

keeping your mind relaxed and open.
Does the crystal have a sound, a taste;
can you feel its life force? Breathe it in
while holding it to your heart and third
eye, and feel the connection. Some
people like to carry a new crystal in their
pocket or a pouch, and hold it as often
as they can. Why not sleep with it under
the pillow or by your side? Attuning
oneself to all new crystals is said to
enhance their ability to assist in healing.

DEDICATING A CRYSTAL
Healers dedicate crystals to begin
bringing their raw energy into focus, a
bit like light converging through a
camera lens, and to align that energy
with those spiritual powers they believe
in. It is thought that the clarity and love
in a heartfelt dedication provides a

context and direction for the healing power of the crystal in all work done with it, and it is a vital part of preparing your crystals.

You can dedicate crystals according to your beliefs and principles. This may be Divine Power, God or the Tao, healing, or simply for the good of all beings. Making a dedication is a simple ceremony that prepares both the user and the crystal for the work to come. Close your eyes, take the crystal in both hands, centre and breathe deeply, feeling your heart opening with love. Now say a short prayer or heartfelt wish, for example: "May this crystal and all the work I do with it be for the good of all beings".

PROGRAMMING A CRYSTAL

After dedication, crystals are often 'programmed' to place a more specific and personal intention within them and to gather their energy into even tighter focus. You can think of it as using the potential of a computer by writing software for a particular application. As many healers believe minerals are living beings, they will usually ask the stone if it is happy to work with their intention. If your crystal does not seem comfortable with your programme, trust your intuition. It may have a different purpose that you will discover later and for which it is more suited.

Begin by requesting that any unwanted past programmes not aligned with your purpose be released. Now, think about what you would like to use the crystal for. Is it general healing: The welfare of your home or family? Bringing more pleasure or friendship into your life? To help you sleep better? To resolve a difficult issue with a loved one? To assist in meditation, or remembering your dreams?

Choose any purpose that is meaningful to you, nothing is too big or too small, providing it serves the highest good of yourself and others, so let your heart and imagination have a free rein.

Sitting quietly, with the crystal held at the third eye, and breathing deeply and freely, focus on your intention, and say a simple prayer or statement that is

meaningful to you. For example:
"Through the power of love and light, I programme this crystal to assist me in sleeping well".

While holding the crystal, imagine yourself sleeping peacefully and waking refreshed, adding the power of visualisation to the programming. The crystal can then be placed under your pillow or by the bedside at night.

Many crystals seem to be happy to hold several programmes, and these can be added to or changed as you wish. However, some people prefer to keep special crystals for just one programme. You will discover which feels right for your as you gather experience.

If crystals are placed in a shared space, it

is best to make sure everybody is comfortable with this. If you are programming a crystal for the healing of somebody else, always ask that person's permission first. We may not always be aware of what is best for others, or ourselves, so some people like to finish all their intentions, dedications and programmes with the phrase:

"In accordance with the highest good of all."

This will neutralise anything that is not going to serve well, or might interfere with another's process.

These principles about choosing, cleansing, nurturing and programming stones are considered fundamental rules in effective crystal healing. If you want to work with crystals, you should always keep them in mind and they will help you develop a rewarding and healing relationship with the mineral kingdom.

LIFE-ENHANCING
CRYSTALS

Like charity, crystal healing often begins at home. If you are attracted to the mineral kingdom, and have learned the basic principles about caring for and using crystals, you begin to discover the thousand and one ways they can enhance all aspects of your own life, and the lives of those you love. The list is endless, and as your confidence and awareness grows, you will discover more and more uses.

As always with crystals, a little is said to go a long way, so cost need not be an issue. One small **quartz** or **amethyst** cluster placed with loving intent within a room can transform it. Here are a few ways to begin bringing crystals into your life.

WEARING CRYSTALS

These days many people are choosing to wear crystals and gem stones as jewellery, feeling this is a great way to let the minerals touch every aspect of their lives. Although people have worn crystals for thousands of years, modern cultures may have lost touch with the traditional meaning and power of this, or perhaps they have used such jewellery simply as symbols of their wealth, power or prestige.

It is believed to be important to let go of too materialistic an attitude to gemstones in order to fully connect with their healing potential. Still, we all recognise the power of a wedding ring, a christening bracelet, a special pendant to mark an anniversary, or a piece of jewellery lovingly passed on from

mother to daughter, all these represent
the meaning of gemstones in everyday
life

Jewellery can touch the world with
beauty, and is believed by crystal
healers to do much more. Sadly, in
many cultures only women wear
jewellery. Although fashion is changing
these days, some men may still feel a
little reluctant to wear a pendant or a
crystal set in a ring or a bracelet. But
remember that until the nineteenth
century men were frequently
bejewelled, and the male of many
species is more colourful than the
female. To bow to convention, one can
wear pendants under clothes, or a
selection of small stones can be placed
in a tiny pouch and hung round the

neck on a leather thong, or carried in a pocket.

It is important to choose, cleanse and dedicate jewellery with as much care and clarity as one would a healing crystal. Cleanse it frequently if wearing it a lot, as the stones may absorb a great deal of stress from a busy life. A single trip on the underground at rush hour may call for a spot of cleansing.

How the stones are mounted, and in which medium, is believed to affect the energy of a piece of jewellery. Crystals set in silver are plentiful and reasonable these days. Gold is said to be an excellent conductor of a crystal's energy, but it is expensive.
A simple leather or silk thong is perfect

for wearing pendants. Many people prefer the stones to be in direct contact with their skin, and may decide not to buy a piece that is backed with metal. This is a matter of personal choice. Whenever choosing a piece of crystal jewellery, you may like to ask yourself and the stone, has it been crafted with respect? Does the mounting enhance or constrict it? Has the crystal been pierced or chipped in some way? Do the stones look happy? Big and expensive is not necessarily best, it is learning when to wear which that is considered far more important, and this is a skill that develops as you grow more familiar with the energy of the stones.

Some people like to pick a piece of

crystal jewellery for a particular purpose, when they may also decide to programme it, or simply because it calls to them. You could choose a pair of earrings to help you hear more perceptively, a pendant to keep you grounded in stressful times, or a small stone to keep in a pouch over the heart to soothe and calm you through the day. Some people like to wear a pouch with tiny stones in the colour of each *chakra* to help them keep their centres balanced and healthy while they are out in the world.

Choose the crystals in pendants thoughtfully, with reference to all you know about a stone's properties and where on the body it is said to work best. For example, **blue lace agate** is said to be best at the throat to help one communicate with clarity and truth, **rose quartz** is considered very soothing and healing for the heart, protecting it and keeping it open. **Citrine** worn around the solar plexus is thought to keep one in touch with one's personal power, and to boost energy levels. A single terminated **clear quartz** pendant facing towards the ground can help drain stressful energy from the body. Pieces crafted in the shape of an animal or coming from a specific tradition, maybe Celtic or Native North American may carry special healing power.

Make sure the stone you are wearing is suitable in its energy. It may not be appropriate to wear a crystal that is believed to be a powerful purger, like

malachite, where you will not feel safe to express any emotions that may be released. A stone that encourages expanded states of awareness would not be appropriate when one needs to be very practical and down-to-earth. Remember, many crystals, particularly **clear quartz**, are believed to amplify the energies around them. One may choose not to wear a large piece of **clear quartz** in an uncomfortable, hectic environment, or one that seems polluted. Some crystals, however, such as **tourmaline**, are said to provide protection in such environments, acting like a shield and deflecting unwanted influences.

Pieces are often programmed by the users to assist in particular ways, for example to bring clarity, patience and dedication in their work, or protection against the pollution of everyday life, or to keep them connected to their centre and essence.

Be creative and thoughtful in how and why you choose your jewellery. A great crystal healer and headmistress of a school has been known to wear a few small crystals in her bra, and some people like to stick one in their shoes if they feel ungrounded. No one needs to know and, visible or invisible, the crystals will be spreading their magic.

Many people like to give crystal jewellery as gifts, feeling it is a great way to touch the people they care for with healing. When you select a piece for a friend, it is considered beneficial to hold a strong intention, focusing on your love for them and whatever special quality might enhance their life at the present moment. Before wrapping the gift, why not spend some time sitting quietly, eyes closed, imagining the friend at his or her most happy and radiant. Holding the jewellery in the right hand (the hand that is said to 'give out' energy) feel in your heart the warm glow of your fondness for this person, and allow it to imbue the crystal. Feel your love travelling from your heart to the palm of your hand. You may experience a warm sensation or imagine a beam of pink light.

It is important to respect others' responsibility for their lives, so make sure a gift is never intrusive. One may feel a friend needs to deal with his or her anger, but it would not be appropriate to choose or programme a crystal to address this without first consulting them. Always use discretion, and your gift may bring much joy and healing. Also remember that some people may be more receptive than others to gemstones, so at first many people choose not to share their special connection with minerals. Whenever possible, however, it is very helpful to pass on the idea of cleansing and nurturing the crystals, simply saying perhaps that they are beautiful, delicate objects than need some tender loving care.

CRYSTALS AROUND THE HOME

Used wisely, crystals are thought to help transform a home into a place of peace, quiet reflection and fun. Have you ever noticed how stuffy a room can feel after you have worked hard in it for a few hours, sitting at a computer? Or how, when hearing bad news, one can feel the room is spinning? Have you felt how sadness or the energy of a row can permeate a room? Crystals are believed to help bring light, joy and balance into any space in which they are thoughtfully placed. Again, a little can go a long way, and you don't need a geological museum to feel their benefits. A small cluster of **clear quartz** is thought to beam sunlight into a whole room. Crystals cannot perform miracles, however, so in times of crisis it is best to seek appropriate help.

Some people like to place **hematite**, or perhaps a beautiful stone they have found in nature, by their front door, asking it to act as guardian of the home. You can gather a basket of small rocks and pebbles to do this also, adding to them as you discover more that appeal.

The modern home is often filled with televisions, computers, microwaves and cell-phones. While this technology has brought incredible benefits, these aids are believed by some people to affect our health in subtle ways with different forms of radiation, and electromagnetic energy. Many stones are prized as helpful in reducing this kind of pollution. Placing a small **amethyst** or **fluorite** on the top of a television, or next to a computer is said to reduce the negative effects of many hours in front of a screen, helping one stay relaxed, refreshed and better able to concentrate. This is believed to be a tough job for a crystal, so check it is not becoming dull or discoloured (said to be sure signs of crystal stress), and cleanse and energise it frequently. One can ask a crystal whether it is happy to do such work, respecting the answer received.

In a bedroom, or a child's room, a small piece of **rose quartz** or delicate **blue lace agate** is believed to bring love and comfort. If a member of your family is recovering from an illness, or just feeling a bit low, a more energising stone, such as **citrine** or **carnelian**, may give support during such a difficult time. To energise and bring light into a room, place four little **clear quartz** single terminators in the corners, pointing upwards (either along the skirting board or a picture rail).

While bearing in mind the suggested properties of the different stones, follow your inspiration and creativity. A special crystal can be placed on a mantelpiece next to a photograph of loved ones, or on a desk to inspire study. Why not choose a crystal to place in your living space to enhance a romantic dinner, or liven up a social gathering?

Some people like to share their feelings with a crystal if they feel sad or lonely. A crystal may provide comfort and reassurance, or help to clarify feelings, or help you to realise what may be preventing you from forming the kind of relationships you would like. You can open your heart to the minerals, speaking your feelings, and listening to their response. You can ask the crystal to provide insight, and help in the release of old patterns that may be limiting, allowing more love and light to flow into your life.

A crystal in the kitchen, the heart of the home, can be a reminder of the sacredness of preparing food and caring for yourself and others. In an age when the food that reaches the table may have been on long, tiring journeys affecting its freshness, why not use a **clear quartz** to cleanse and re-energise vegetables and fruits? This can be done using a simple intention, visualising vital energy flowing into the food.

At the end of a tiring day, it can be soothing to choose a crystal to hold while taking a long bath. If it is a stone that is happy in water, let it sit in the bath, infusing the water with its healing. It may help in releasing any stress and worry you are holding on to.

The possibilities for enhancing the home with crystals are limitless, so express your creativity and intuition, opening yourself to the sensuality and delicacy of the stones. The most important thing is that you enjoy them.

•

CRYSTAL
LAYOUTS
FOR
PERSONAL
HEALING

There are many ways minerals are used in healing, ranging from simply holding and sitting with a stone programmed in a particular way or which carry a certain energy, to the 'laying on' of dozens of crystals over and around the body. As minerals are considered very powerful in affecting our energy, it is a good idea to begin gently. If at any stage you feel unsafe, remove the stones and continue working at a later time.

Perhaps the best ways to experience the potential of crystals is to invest in a session or two with a crystal healer. Choose someone who seems trustworthy and is professionally qualified with some years experience, even if this means saying 'no' to a few people before finding the right one.

There is no obligation, and for the healing to be effective it is vital to trust the healer and feel safe.

If you are using the stones on yourself or other people it is important to prepare yourself and the space in which you will work. Here are some ways to do this:

PREPARING THE HEALING SPACE
A room kept solely for healing, self-development and meditation work is ideal, but most people do not have this luxury, so you might begin by defining a space in some way to use within a room. Use a neutrally decorated area that is free from too much clutter or electrical equipment. You need to be able to relax and focus, so choose a

place where there will be no interruptions, and let others know you are not to be disturbed. Using the same space each time is thought to help build a healing vibration and make it easier to access a centred and relaxed state of being.

Many people like to mark their healing space with a special cloth or rug. It needs to be large enough for the work intended and to spread out the crystals and other tools. You could define your area and set up a 'room within a room' with four small pieces of **amethyst**, **rose quartz** or **clear quartz** terminators placed in each corner. You should programme them to 'hold' the space, allowing only those energies that are helpful to come into it. Direct any unwanted energy to the earth or sun.

Always cleanse these crystals before and after a session.

Always cleanse the space before doing healing work. Some people like to use a bell or gong, or 'smudge' the area with sage or incense, while holding it, and walking around it with the intention to remove unwanted energies. Then dedicate the space, saying for example: "I dedicate this space to the healing of myself and others in accordance with Divine Will and the good of all beings". One can make a prayer, or ask for a blessing.

Bring the crystals to be used into the space once they are clean and ready. Cleanse the space after the session, and the larger room itself.

PREPARING YOURSELF

Before beginning a session it is important to prepare yourself as well as the space and the stones. You can 'smudge' the different *chakras*, your outer body and your hands and feet, paying particular attention to your head, shoulders, back of the neck and the *chakra* points. Some people like to simply sit for a few moments, breathing out tensions and imagining themselves filling with radiant golden light. You can ask for a blessing, guidance and protection according to your beliefs, visualising a loving connection to the higher self or higher wisdom.

Sitting with eyes closed, visualise white light entering in a beam through the crown *chakra*, feeling the breath pulling this light into your body. Alternate this with visualising a rich earthy red entering through the root *chakra*. Imagine these two energies meeting in the heart, filling it with rose-coloured healing light. On the outbreath, let this pink light flow out of your heart, surrounding you in a cocoon of love, peace and protection.

In all crystal work, be focused in your purpose, and always set a clear intention. It is best not to be concerned about a set outcome, however, as such expectations may block the energy, and healing can often come in ways that cannot be anticipated.

If more than one crystal is to be used, see if they seem harmonious and balanced as a group. One may 'attune' them by imagining or requesting them to work together as a team. It is said to be best to let the stones lie directly on the skin for maximum effect. Choose stones that are a suitable shape and size for the part of the body they are to be placed on. For example, a large or jagged piece would not be appropriate for the throat or third eye centre.

BUILDING ON YOUR BASIC SET OF CRYSTALS

When you are using crystals for personal healing you may like to build on the essential crystals listed on page 39-45. Once again these need not be expensive when you begin your more specific healing work. Build on these gradually, perhaps adding larger or more high quality specimens as you discover those that seem most effective. Remember that the relationship between the user and the crystals is personal and dependent on your energy. Here is a reminder of the most popular and frequently used healing crystals, and the *chakra* model of human energy described earlier:

Root *chakra*:
smoky quartz, bloodstone

Sacral *chakra*:
carnelian, tiger's eye

Solar plexus *chakra*:
citrine, amber

Heart *chakra*:
rose quartz, green adventurine

Throat *chakra*:
blue lace agate

Third eye *chakra*:
amethyst, azurite

Crown *chakra*:
amethyst, clear quartz

4 small clear quartz single terminators
4 small clear quartz double terminators
2 medium clear quartz single terminators

One stone for each *chakra* is sufficient initially. Such a set will allow one to do all the following healing practices, including a full *chakra* layout.

❧

PROGRAMMING CRYSTALS FOR HEALING

Many healers like to programme a set of stones for *chakra* healing, keeping these solely for this purpose. This is believed to increase their healing potency, which will strengthen with each use. As you gather more crystals, you can keep stones programmed to work in layouts just for that purpose. Healers stress the importance of programming all crystals used in healing and self-development, so their energy is focused for maximum effect.

HARMONISING MALE/FEMALE SIDES

Research has shown that the left (governing the right side of the body) and the right (governing the left side of the body) hemispheres of the brain have specialised abilities. The right side of the brain appears to operate more intuitively, artistically and laterally, the left more rationally and logically. Most people; however, appear to be more left or right-brained.

Use two single or double terminated **clear quartz** to help balance this aspect of our energy, sometimes known as the female and male or yin and yang. This will harmonise intuitive and rational capacities, both of which are needed to create and manifest our highest potential. This can be done as a daily tonic to help physical and emotional wellbeing. It is a great way to start or finish the day, to prepare for a special project or creative task, to centre ourselves if we feel out of sorts, and prior to meditation or a healing session.

Sit comfortably, where you will not be disturbed, and place one crystal in the left (receiving) palm with the termination pointed towards the wrist, and the other crystal in your right (giving out) palm, with the termination facing away from the wrist. This helps create a circular flow of energy that is said to help purify, realign and energise. Let the tip of your tongue rest gently on the roof of your mouth, as this is believed to 'connect up' the energy lines between the body and head (a bit like an electrical switch), helping the flow of vital energy or 'chi' between them. Now sit quietly and relax for 10 to 15 minutes. Don't forget to cleanse the **quartz** when you have finished, and to drink some water.

CHAKRA BALANCING LAYOUT

This is a full *chakra*-balancing layout. Some people like to begin by placing just one or two stones on those centres they feel drawn to work with, increasing to a full layout as they familiarise themselves with the process and the effects of such work.

Gather the crystals to be used and sit with them, attuning them to each other and yourself, and requesting their help in the healing, setting the intention to bring the *chakras* into balance. It is a good idea to lay them out in the order they will be used so they come easily to hand when you lie down.

Beginning at the root *chakra*, place your left hand over it and contact the energy there, inviting the centre and body to open, receive healing and come into balance, then gently place the chosen stone.

Move up the body centre by centre to the crown. If the stone to be used at the crown is terminated, let the tip face upward, with the crystal leaning against the top of the head. Now relax and let the crystals work. There is no need to do anything. Stay resting for

20 to 30 minutes. You can set an alarm clock to go off after a certain time, as one can fall asleep quite easily as the crystals are working. Why not try playing some inspiring music to help you relax and let go? Some people may experience different thoughts, emotions, memories or images arising as their energy responds to the crystals. Sometimes there may be a release of pent-up emotion. This is part of the healing, and it is best to relax and simply allow the energy to move through one, as much as possible without involvement or attachment, but simply being a witness. However, if you feel unsafe or distressed, you may gently bring the healing to a close.

When time is up, remove the stones

softly and slowly. One can begin at the crown, moving down to the root, or remove the crystals in any order that feels right intuitively. Some people like to leave the heart or solar plexus stone till last. After removing the crystals, spend a few moments breathing into the legs with your hands on the solar plexus, to ground and fully return to the body. Cleanse and thank the stones, and drink plenty of water to help any toxins released to be flushed out.

PYRAMID REGENERATION LAYOUT

This layout is believed to create a powerful field of energy of a very high vibration, drawing the transformative power of light into one's being, and helping release old tensions and blockages. Always prepare yourself and your space very carefully beforehand, asking for guidance and protection according to your beliefs, and setting a clear intention that it be for your healing and for the highest good of all. Four small double terminated **clear quartz** crystals are needed. Double terminated **quartz** is used so that one end can draw out old energy, while the other end can infuse the body with fresh energy.

Lay the crystals in the form of an equal four-sided pyramid, with one at the head, one at the feet, and the others

Pyramid Regeneration Layout

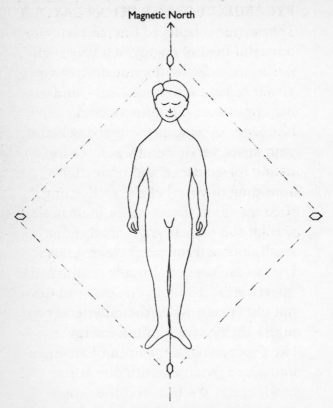

Magnetic North

Lay four double terminated clear quartz crystals in the form of the base of a pyramid, as shown below, ensuring the pyramid and body are aligned with magnetic North either side of the palms of the hands. (see diagram opposite) Ensure that your head and feet are aligned with magnetic North. Lay the crystals down so that one termination is faced away from the body and the other is pointing into the body. Visualise the sides of the pyramid reaching up to the apex above you, imagining light and healing energy showering down from the top. Again, place the tip of your tongue to the roof of your mouth, and then simply close your eyes and rest for 10 to 15 minutes, or as long as feels necessary. Take a few deep breaths into the solar plexus, legs and feet when you have finished, to ensure that you are grounded. Cleanse the crystals as usual, and drink some water.

EASING EMOTIONAL AND MENTAL STRESS

We may experience times when we feel temporarily burdened with worry or emotion. Tension headaches and migraines can be a common reaction to such pressure, perhaps due to excess energy that is not able to find an outlet. **Amethyst** may be used to gently stabilise the energy, helping to deflect any negativity; **citrine** is said to centre and boost our energy; **rose quartz** to ease and calm the heart; and **amber** to soothe and settle us.

Fluorite is particularly prized for its ability to bring order to fluxing mental and emotional states, helping us access a higher understanding of our process. You can place **purple fluorite** at the third eye, and **green fluorite** at the solar plexus and sacral *chakra*, while holding two **clear quartz** (as in the clearing and energising exercise, p123) to ease a troubled mind and heart.

Some relief from headaches and migraines may be gained by placing the left hand upon the head at the point of pain, while the right holds a **clear quartz** single terminator. With the point of the crystal facing away from the wrist, hold the intention of releasing unwanted energy to the sun or earth, visualising this moving out of the crystal as you direct it away from the body. Visualise the unwanted energy as dirty smoke or fast flowing muddy water.

If symptoms persist consult a doctor or the appropriate professional. Most healers agree crystals are best used as a complimentary therapy, not as a replacement for orthodox treatments.

MORE WAYS
TO USE
CRYSTALS
FOR HEALING
AND SELF-
DEVELOPMENT

Those who are interested in Feng Shui (the 5000 year old Chinese system of harmonising the energy in our homes and workplaces) may like to explore programming crystals to place in particular areas of their environments to enhance the different energies there.

Again, it is recommended, if possible, that these special crystals are kept only for their designated purpose, and many people prefer not to have them touched by others. This is a matter of personal choice, so trust your intuition in this regard.

~

MEDITATION AND CRYSTALS

Meditation is aimed at clearing and quieting the mind in order to expand beyond its conceptual limits, and leading to the re-experiencing of oneself as greater than the body, mind and emotions. It is a prized practice of personal and spiritual development for many people around the world, and is said to bring benefits such as stress reduction, greater focus and clarity of thought, improved memory and concentration, enhanced creativity and the ability to relax more easily. Learning to access a meditative state can be one of the finest gifts we can give ourselves and may lead to much positive change.

Meditation may involve complex visualisation and concentration exercises, or simply sitting still and 'keeping quiet'. Why not invest in a book or some classes to explore which style might suit you, and the benefits to be gained? When you begin to meditate, many thoughts, feelings and images may arise unasked. It is important not to suppress these (this will only strengthen them or cause mental strain), but rather, as much as possible, 'witness' their passing without attachment or interference. One can ask the question "Who is experiencing this thought?" or "In whom is this emotion arising?" Some people like to simply sit quietly, asking, "Who is in?" or "Who is meditating?"

Many teachers advise meditating for no more than ten minutes when you begin, increasing the time as feels comfortable. Keeping to the same place and time is said to help the mind and body respond more easily and charges the meditation space with enhancing vibrations. As in healing, it is important to let go of the desire for a particular outcome. Relax, the paradox is the less you 'do', the more effective meditation will be.

∾

Certain minerals are used to enhance meditative experiences. **Amethyst** can be placed on the third eye to help calm the mind, leading it towards releasing its ego-centred boundary to experience

something greater. **Fluorite** pyramids
are said to be wonderful aids, allowing
the mind to access its deeper
knowledge of universal spiritual truth,
including oneness with all of creation.

~

Perhaps the most popular crystal used
in meditation is **clear quartz**. It is
believed to infuse the body with pure
light containing all the healing colours
of the rainbow. Channelling crystals
have been used to communicate with
one's higher self or guides. Many people
like to dedicate and programme special
clear **quartz** just for meditation.

Hold the crystal chosen while meditating, or place it in front of you, preferably at third eye level. Attune to the mineral before beginning each session. You can breathe in the energy of the crystal and ask for its assistance.

∿

Meditating with a crystal can be a wonderful way to discover information about its properties and how it can assist in one's transformation. It may be best to use only those stones that are gentle in action and with which you are familiar. Stones such as **malachite** or **azurite** may initiate an experience that is too strong or causes discomfort. Treat the power of the crystals with respect.

AFFIRMATIONS AND VISUALISATION

You can use crystals to enhance the effectiveness of visualisations and affirmations. These healing techniques draw on the latent power of the subconscious mind to plant positive seeds in the form of images or statements that can grow and help release thoughts or feelings that may be hindering your life experience. Crystals may be used to hold and transmit life-enhancing visions of your highest possibility and truth, infusing your body, heart and mind, and 'weeding out' negativity.

For example, if you want to enhance a feeling of confidence in social situations, you might programme a **clear quartz** crystal by holding it at the third eye while imagining yourself interacting naturally and happily. You might repeat an affirmation such as "I am loved and wanted for who I am" at the same time. This crystal could then be worn in difficult social situations, reflecting back the positive image and statement. Such crystals can be used to gain insight into the roots of a difficulty and guidance as to how to begin healing. Simply hold the stone in meditation or quiet time, requesting its assistance. **Clear quartz** is usually favoured for this kind of work.

It is considered important to include the phrase "for the good of all beings"

with such programming, as you may
not fully understand the reasons for so-
called 'negative' feelings, which may in
the longer term lead to great
understanding and evolution.

❧

MASSAGE AND CRYSTALS
Massage can be a great way to nourish
and love our bodies and ourselves, and
crystals can used to bring added
healing to the power of touch.
Choose stones that are smooth and
comfortable to hold, and feel good on
the body. Polished **quartz** with smooth
bases designed for this purpose can
sometimes be found. A crystal ball is
wonderful to use, and the circular
shape is said to carry the added

symbolic power of wholeness. Egg-shaped crystals are prized for their nurturing, feminine and protective qualities.

§

There are many ways to massage yourself and gentle intuitive touch can be wonderfully healing even if one doesn't have specialist knowledge. However, a short course is recommended if you want to practise on others. It is important to understand how to apply pressure safely in deep massage. However, for self-massage, connect to your heart's intelligence, and work with love. Why not programme some crystals especially for this purpose? You can work in circles over the whole body, easing tensions and any soreness. This can be a great way to work over the stomach, abdomen and intestines, and also around the diaphragm. All these areas may have a build up of tension and stagnant energy. If you know about the energy or 'meridian' lines of the body (used in techniques such as shiatsu or acupuncture) you can trace these with the tip of a crystal, programming it to assist in clearing and encouraging the flow of energy.

Try examining the aura with your left hand for areas that need or want massage. You could ask for guidance from your higher self or intuition. Pass your hand over the body one to two inches from the skin. You may discover areas where you feel resistance, or a change in energy (a cold or hot spot, or the feeling of a 'hole'). Listen to the body, and what it needs.

❧

Crystals recommended for massage again include **clear quartz**, **amethyst**, and **fluorite**. All these stones infuse the body with their special properties. **Bloodstone** is said to be excellent for the intestines and abdomen due to its capacity to cleanse the physical organs and help circulation. Experiment gently, and be creative, drawing on what you know of the *chakras* and the properties of different crystals.

For example, you can massage your body in section relating to these *chakras*, using the coloured stones recommended. Some people like to combine such massage with colour breathing.

For example, as you work over the solar plexus, on the in-breath visualise a beautiful, vibrant yellow flooding the centre, gently easing out blocked energy and opening it like a flower, and on the out-breath, imagine releasing any tension and unwanted energy.

If you use massage oils, why not 'charge' them with crystal energy. Simply place a cleansed crystal, programmed with a healing intention into the oil and leave it for 24 hours in sunlight or moonlight. Oil charged with **citrine** may help with stomach cramp or indigestion, or **amethyst** charged oil with stress and worry.

CRYSTAL ELIXIRS

An elixir is purified water charged with crystal energy and believed to carry the vibration of the stone into the body to circulate. It is best to use distilled water free from any pollutants and held in a glass container. Simply place the programmed crystal into the water and leave in the sun or moonlight for 24 hours. Moon elixirs are particularly recommended for working on emotional issues. Once charged, place the liquid in a well-labelled dark container.

❧

Elixirs are believed to be very energising so use them sparingly. A few drops at a time in a glass of water or under the tongue two to three times a day are plenty. Do not take them too frequently, and if you find their effect is too strong, stop.

◆

USING A PENDULUM FOR HEALING

A pendulum is a small crystal (a **quartz** octahedron works well) or object placed on a chain or thong so it can swing freely. Some people make their own with a key or ring. You can often find beautiful ones in crystal shops. Using a technique called 'dowsing', you can ask the pendulum different questions about anything requiring only a 'yes' or 'no' answer. For example, whether a food or drink is healthy for you to eat or whether you should work on a particular *chakra* or in a particular way. Some people say a pendulum provides a bridge between and amplifies one's intuition and inner knowing.

৬৯

To establish a pendulum's responses: hold it in your left hand (though some people may prefer to use the right hand) at arm's length from your body. Ask it to indicate its movement for 'yes' (often a clockwise circle), its movement for 'no' (often an anti-clockwise circle) and 'don't know' (often stationary or an up and down movement). Check before each session how it is going to respond, as the way it answers can change. You can use the other hand to touch or hold whatever the question may refer to, although you may ask questions about anything you choose whether physically present or not.

For a pendulum to give accurate answers, it is important to be detached from the outcome of a question while asking it, or it is possible to bias the response with one's conscious mind. Always check a response with your own intuition and common sense.

Once you have gained experience with the pendulum, and learned to trust its responses, some people like to use them to work more deeply with the *chakras*, for example to ask whether a *chakra* is balanced, congested, under-energised or overcharged. A more advanced method is to ask which other *chakras* may need working on to bring a certain centre into balance. No *chakra* works in isolation, and an imbalance in one may have its roots in another. Use the checklist overleaf for a suggested way to discover more about the health of the *chakras* using the pendulum,

once one has gained sufficient experience
and is confident of its responses:
(see checklist of questions for pendulum
opposite).

ℒ

Depending on the answers received,
work to reduce or increase the energy in
a centre by discharging or charging it.
Choose crystals appropriate to the
chakra or *chakras* to be worked on. Place
these on the centre, and at each side of
the main *chakra*, a small single
terminated **quartz** crystal. To discharge
or release congestion in a centre, place
the **quartz** terminations away from the
stone, to charge a centre place them

148

Working with the Chakras using a pendulum

Using the pendulum, go through each chakra asking whether it is balanced, congested, underenergised or overenergised. Once a 'yes' answer is received, mark this on the form. One can also go through the centres listed underneath this chakra, asking one by one if the centre needs work to bring the first one into balance. This may vary from none to several. When one is working to discharge or charge the main chakra, one can then lay an appropriate stone on the other centres indicated by the pendulum, placing clear quartz double terminators between them to assist energy flow (see example in diagram on page151).

Centre	root	sacral	solar plexus	heart	third eye	crown
balanced						
congested						
underenergised						
overenergised						

Work on these centre

root   sacral   solar plexus   heart   throat   third eye   crown towards the stone. You can place stones on the other *chakras* not being directly worked on to encourage an overall balancing, or on the few indicated by the pendulum. You can also place small double terminated clear **quartz** crystals between the *chakras* worked on to encourage the flow of energy between them (see Diagram opposite):

While working on individual *chakra*, some people like to 'dialogue' with the centres, much as one would with a friend one was getting to know. You can invite the centre to give feedback, asking questions and listening for any response that may come. Using your intuition, it is believed to be possible to discover powerful visualisations and affirmations that can be used to heal

More in-depth work on Chakras

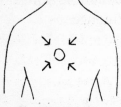

Charging a chakra

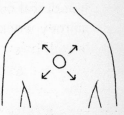

Discharging a chakra

In both cases, place the chosen stone on the centre, surrounding it with four single terminated clear quartz crystals in the direction shown above.

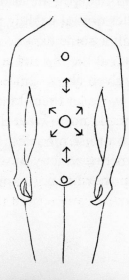

Discharging an overenergised solar plexus, with stones placed on the heart and root chakra on the basis of information received using the pendulum checklist (see page 149), and connected up with double terminated clear quartz.

old wounds at these centres. This is a wonderful technique to explore as you gain experience, and confidence.

WORKING ON OTHERS
You may find that you are asked or drawn to offer crystal healing to friends and family after some experience has been gained. All the layouts and suggestions given above can be offered to others. Always let them know if you are experienced and to what degree, and do not promise miracles. Never pressure someone to let you work on him or her if they are not happy for you to do so.

Again, it is considered critical not to be attached to a particular outcome, but to realise one is simply a channel for healing energy. This can be difficult if you are working with those close to you. If you cannot work on someone without wanting or feeling responsible for a certain result, then it may be best not to work with them.

Do not offer to diagnose someone's difficulty or problem, even if asked, as this is a very complex process and one can easily misinform them or set them worrying unnecessarily.

Before you begin working on another person, set the intention that you will not take on any unwanted energy from them. Some people like to visualise a strong healing light about them, for example pink or gold, to protect them while them open themselves as a channel for healing. Always work with love and non-judgementally, allowing the other person to be responsible for their healing.

~

Make the person comfortable, and let them ask any questions they want to. Invite them to give feedback of their experience during the healing if it helps them. Always be ready to listen, but do not feel you need to provide 'expert' responses. Stay relaxed and trust the process.

❦

Once the healing is complete, make sure the person is fully grounded and settled. Sometimes a sweet biscuit or fruit drink can help.

❧

Another way to work with others is through absent healing. Here it is believed you can offer healing to another wherever they are in the world. Simply programming a crystal with a healing intention or vision of them and placing this over their picture is said to work well. One can set up a small pyramid within which to place crystals, pictures, healing visions, prayers and blessings for the person concerned.

Pyramids are believed to offer a strong geometric energy that amplifies the power of anything within it. Using four single terminated **clear quartz** crystals pointing inwards to the centre (further charging the pyramid) to form the base, visualise the four sides rising inwards to the apex of the pyramid, creating a solid form of love and light. Remember that one must always get permission before offering absent healing so as not to interfere with another's freedom of will. Always ask first and respect the other person's wishes.

SOME
FINAL
WORDS

My prayer is that this book has given you some insight into the amazing beauty and healing potential of minerals, and provided sound principles upon which to begin developing your ability as a crystal healer. While many claims are made for their power, it may be wiser to discover one's own truth through exploring and experiencing their energy, and forming one's own opinion. In time, you may choose to take a course in crystal healing. It can be wonderful to share experiences, and it will develop your confidence and skill if you should want to work on others.

℀

Crystals have been part of this planet for far longer than mankind, and in drawing on their healing power I believe we reconnect with the sacred traditions of our ancestors, and are encouraged to experience ourselves as evolving, self-determining beings, operating in harmony with the natural world.

If you continue to practise crystal healing, you will find your understanding of yourself, others and the crystal kingdom expanding and deepening, and yet there will always be more to learn and discover.

Work patiently, with a loving heart, and with respect for all of life.

✦

May the mineral kingdom support you in manifesting your dream, and in becoming all that you wish to be?